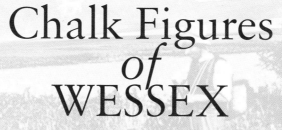

Chalk Figures
of
WESSEX

by
Kent Goodman

Since the days long, long ago, when hunter-gatherer tribes created beautiful, sinuous works of art upon cave walls, mankind has had an irresistible urge to leave an impression on his surroundings. Perhaps it was done for religious reasons, to please the gods or seek their intervention; perhaps to mark ownership of a territory, by using the image of a Great Ancestor or tribal totem; or perhaps it was commemorative of an important event.

It seems fitting that an off-shoot of this artistic leaning, the rather strange and mysterious art of carving giant hill figures, should occur most frequently in Wessex. This small area of the world has been home to the strange and mysterious for untold generations – rings of stone, flying saucers, burial chambers, witchcraft and crop circles. The latter could even be called a modern example of hill figures, land art on a somewhat smaller scale, and at least less permanent basis.

There are examples of hill figures throughout the world. The Nazca lines in Peru, the Great Snake in America, but this type of art is predominately found in Wessex. Besides the general ambience of the area, this part of western England has also been chosen because of the large number of suitable hills, green with turf on the outside, white with chalk on the inside, available for use as canvases. There have been quite an assortment of figures to adorn these softly undulating hills, including military badges, a panda, a kiwi, a naked giant and of course, plenty of horses.

The Uffington White Horse

Inset:
This painting of the Uffington White Horse by Wiltshire artist Peter Collyer illustrates how the earliest hill figures were created to blend in with the contours of the landscape.

Opposite page:
The Uffington White Horse is by far the oldest hill figure in Wessex. It was probably cut late in the first century AD by the local Celtic tribe as a totem and territorial marker.

The enigmatic hill figure of the Uffington White Horse, undoubtedly the most famous 'horse', can be seen anywhere in the Vale, from Swindon to Abingdon, although it can't be viewed up close. It is situated on the northern escarpment of the Berkshire Downs above Uffington hamlet. The ancient earthwork of Uffington Castle crowns the top of the hill. This horse has been gracing White Horse Hill for at least 900 years. A book in the 12th century mentioned an accompanying foal, but if there ever was one, it has long since disappeared. The horse has long been considered remarkable. For example, in the 14th century it was considered the second wonder of the world, with Stonehenge being the first.

Legends of giants are in evidence by the names of geographical features. The glacial tiers below the horse are known as the Giant's Stairs, and a deep combe nearby is called the Manger. Not far from the horse is the ancient Neolithic chambered long barrow called Wayland's Smithy. Named after a Norse god, it was said that if a person left his horse outside the tomb, and also left a payment of a groat, in the morning the horse would be shod. Wayland was also supposed to have shod the Uffington horse. Certainly, a white horse was the emblem of the Saxons, and so some felt that it was carved on the orders of Hengist, the Saxon chieftain, about 1500 years ago. However, their horse is depicted standing on its heels, facing left. This one faces right and appears to be running. Of course, another theory was that King Alfred ordered it to be carved to celebrate his victory at Ashdown in 871. Like the Bratton horse, it was likely to have been created much earlier, since the outline resembles horses on early Iron Age coins, which would coincide with the fort on the hill. The most likely explanation is that it was a totem for the local people like the Belgae, perhaps cut late in the first century AD. Its flowing style corresponds with Celtic art styles, so that provides a clue as to the makers. The Romans wouldn't have allowed the native people to create such a totem, so that shows us that it must have been carved before the occupation. However, there is a final clue that suggests that the flowing art style was also widespread in areas like Scandinavia since the Bronze Age, so the horse could be much older still.

There is a flat area towards the bottom of White Horse Hill known as Dragon's Hill, the spot where St George slew the dragon. The saint himself is a continuation from an earlier pagan deity, probably a horse-god.

The art of cutting white horses was described by Morris Marples in 1949 as *leucippotomy*. 'For there is a real need for some such short expression to cover the cutting of all such figures, and it is inconvenient to have to use a descriptive phrase every time.' This ancient craft involves marking out the design first, following the orders of someone a way off, who shouts directions. Then the top layer of turf is cut to get at the white chalk underneath. 'However, it is often not bright enough, in which case the figure is excavated to a depth of about two feet, and fresh white chalk, quarried nearby, is pounded on top. A circular area of turf is left for the eye. If the figure is in outline only, then a trench of two feet wide and two feet deep in excavated. Once cut, the figure is visible for miles.' However, it won't stay in that condition for long, and many horses and other totems have been lost over the years through neglect.

The figure has to be rescoured occasionally or it will revert to grass. This has, in the past, taken place approximately every seven years. The rescouring was usually an occasion of great feasting, drinking, gaming and gaiety that went on for days, and was paid for by the lord of the manor. In modern times, that duty has fallen to The National Trust and the Department of the Environment, among others.

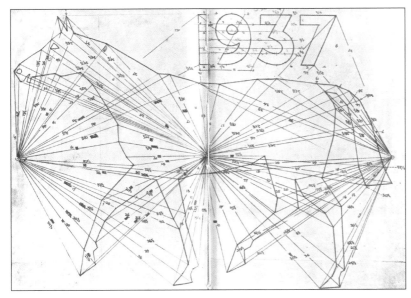

Bratton, or Westbury White Horse

The Bratton, or Westbury White Horse is best viewed from the B3098 to Bratton, off the A360 Devizes–Amesbury road. This is the oldest horse in Wiltshire, made in 1778. It was cut by Mr Gee, Steward to Lord Abingdon. He didn't like the artistic merits of the original horse so he destroyed it when creating the new one, which is now made of concrete, not chalk.

On a good clear day you can also see the Cherhill and Alton Barnes horses from here. The original horse had stood on the same spot since at least 1066. It was, legend states, carved to celebrate King Alfred's victory over the Danes at Ethandun in 878. Since there is also an Iron Age hillfort (Bratton Camp) above the horse, it may be more likely that it was a totem for the tribe that lived in the area. This early example of hill carving was more in the shape of a dog, with a long body and short legs. It also wore a saddle blanket decorated with a number of crescent designs. Even its long tail that curved upwards ended in the traditional Celtic symbol of fertility – the crescent moon.

Cherhill White Horse

The Cherhill White Horse is best viewed from the A4 Marlborough to Bath road. This horse also has a hillfort (Oldbury Castle) on top, although there is nothing to suggest that it replaced anything older. It was carved in 1780 by men working under orders from Dr Alsop of Calne, known as the 'mad doctor', who shouted orders through a megaphone from the bottom of the hill. It used to have the bottoms of glass bottles for its eyes, but souvenir hunters kept taking them. The Lansdowne Obelisk near it was erected in 1845 by Lord Lansdowne to celebrate his ancestor Sir William Petty.

Cerne Abbas Giant

The Cerne Abbas Giant is best viewed from the A352. Measuring 180 feet from head to foot, it overlooks the ancient village of Cerne Abbas in Dorset. It was presented to the National Trust by the son of General Pitt-Rivers in 1920, and was endowed by Sir Henry Hoare of Stourhead four years later, guaranteeing its upkeep. The giant's right hand holds a knobby club that is 120 feet long. He also sports a 20 foot long erect phallus (although some recent reports suggest that this has grown since earlier times, when there may have been a navel), which gives him the nickname Rude Man of Cerne. His ribs, nipples, chest muscles and facial features are also delineated. This hill figure is in outline only, made from a ditch two feet wide and two feet deep. In 18th century literature, reference was made to three illegible letters placed below the giant, and over them three other letters or numerals. The numbers might have been 798, and the letters may by IHS, or the Greek for Jesus. He was undoubtedly associated with fertility, especially since on May Day, a traditional time for fertility rites, the phallus points directly at the rising sun. At one time the village maypole was positioned in an enclosure not far from the giant's left hand in an area called the Trendle or Frying Pan. One theory is that during pagan times when human sacrifice was practised, the victims were held in this area until their time was due. The term 'frying pan' could also have been used because the villagers identified the giant with Beelzebub in the old Mummers' Christmas play, in which he says:

> Here come I, Beelzebub
> And over my shoulders I carry my club
> And in my hand a frying pan
> And I think myself a jolly old man.

The earliest written account of the Giant was in 1751. This is used to prove that the Giant, although old, is not ancient. The account, by the Reverend John Hutchins, mentions him in his guide to Dorset. He said the locals told him it had been erected in 1539, the year the monastery was dissolved. The figure was supposed to represent the nasty abbot Thomas Corton, with the phallus suggesting his lustful ways, the club his vicious revenge on those who annoyed him and his feet pointing away from the village to show he had been driven out. However, the Giant wasn't mentioned in a guide in 1617 or an earlier one of 1356. The monks in the area were certainly tolerant, for in 1268 they actually made a representation of the pagan god Priapus, because the country folks' cows had become diseased.

Above:
A computer generated reproduction of the Cerne Abbas Giant.

Left:
The Cerne Abbas giant has been renowned for hundreds of years as an aid to fertility for obvious reasons. He is most likely meant to be a depiction of Hercules, possibly created around AD 190 when the Emperor Commodius set up a cult based on the god.

Gigantic Legends – fact or fancy?

T he figure might have been the work of the Clubmen or Club Risers, groups of farm labourers who banded together, especially in 1644 and 1645 to prevent Civil War soldiers from looting. They were armed with clubs and often gathered at traditional places, like Badbury Rings. At Godmaston, between Cerne and Dorchester, a serious clash between the Clubmen and soldiers resulted in several deaths. In 1645 about 10,000 were gathered to face Cromwell (but they disbanded).

However, most people still like to think it's very old. So who is it? Perhaps he was Nodens, a Celtic god of the Durotriges tribe who lived in the area before the Romans, or Succellos, The Good Striker. A bronze handle of Celtic origin has been found that has the figure of a naked man on it (Nodens), in a style similar to the Giant. Others suggest that it is Hercules, popular especially after the Emperor Commodius set up a cult in AD 191, with himself as a reincarnation of the god. In 1764 Stukeley wrote that the local people referred to the Giant as Helis. Another writer stated that until the 6th century the god Helith was worshipped. These could be bastardisations of the ancient version of Hercules, Helethkin. It has also been suggested that the figure was once accompanied by a dog, now pretty much invisible.

In his left hand once hung something, either a hare, signifying the hunt (Nodens) or a lion skin, a Hercules trademark. The latter seemed to win the day when a resistivity test in 1979 showed what appeared to be a lion skin outline.

Young ladies wishing to keep their lovers should walk around him and to get pregnant, spend a night on him. Morris Men celebrate May Day by dancing on him in the early hours of the morning. It was said that the local people found a real giant on the spot sleeping off the effects of eating an over-abundance of sheep, and killed him, marking his outline. The Marquis of Bath visited the Giant after failing to father any children, and later his daughter was born. He and his wife made pilgrimages to it many times afterwards. A legend says that at the end of the 6th century, Saint Augustine came to Cerne with other missionaries to convert the local heathens, who instead tied cows' tails to their robes and hounded them out of the village. He called on God, who caused the children of the village to be born with tails, and so they took him back, and he founded the Abbey of Cernel, from the Latin cerno (I see) and Hebrew El (God). From this legend it could be inferred that there was a particularly stubborn brand of paganism in the area.

Above:

Early depictions of the Giant included strange writing between his legs, and omitted his most famous attribute.

Right:

The square enclosure above the Giant is known as the Frying Pan, perhaps because of folk memories of early gruesome sacrifices that may have taken place there.

Gog and Magog, known as the last of the tribe of giants in the old days, were carved into the hillside below the Citadel in Plymouth (the carvings cannot be seen today). Records as far back as the 1400s record the scouring of two giants, one bigger than the other, each brandishing clubs. The bigger one was later identified with Corineus, the Cornish giant, who fought Gogmagog in a battle. He threw the latter into the ocean at Goemagot's Leap. According to the story, in the old days Corineus was given the province of Cornwall, and he was happy to have it, even though it had become the home of giants who had been expelled from other parts. He was happy partly because he loved to fight and kill them. Amongst the giants was one, according to Geoffrey of Monmouth, writing about 1140, 'by name of Goemagot, twelve cubits in height, who was of such lustihood that when he had once uprooted it, he would wield an oak tree as lightly as it were a wand of hazel'. As it happened, all the giants were killed except this one, whom Corineus wanted to wrestle. And this he did, 'making the very air quake with their breathless gasping'. When Goemagot managed to break three of Corineus' ribs, he became very angry and lifting the giant on his shoulders, flung him into the sea, 'where, falling on the sharp rocks, he was mangled all to pieces and dyed the waves with his blood.'

Gog and Magog

Below:

Two of Britain's best known giants, Gog and Magog, used to be seen on the turf near Plymouth Hoe. The pair were also depicted in Cambridge and can still be seen on London's Guildhall. Here they are given the comic treatment in an early illustration for Punch *magazine.*

WESTBURY

Above:

The Westbury White Horse is the oldest in Wiltshire. Like many other hill figures, it was cut next to an ancient hillfort – in this case, Bratton Camp.

All the English hill-figures except four are in the chalk country of the south. Of the seventeen horses, eleven are actually within the comparatively narrow area of Wessex. Wessex in general (and Wiltshire in particular) has long been associated with horses, going back at least as far as the ancient Celts, well known for their cult of the horse, and the earliest white horses were probably cut by people who worshipped the horse goddess Epona (or Estonia). A large number of the hill figures are built close to ancient earthworks and trackways, thus leading us to believe that they were primarily used as territorial markers.

There are many folk-tales and traditions concerning horses. For instance, farmers would often hang stones that had natural holes in them, called hagstones, in the stables to protect the animals from disease and spells. An unmarried girl would count the number of white horses she saw until she reached one hundred. Then the first man she shook hands with after that would end up as her husband. However, it was unlucky for a woman to be present when a mare gave birth. And a mare in foal would never be used to pull a coffin, or else the mare or foal or both would die. One horse charm still in use today is the horseshoe, considered magical in ancient times partly because it looks like the crescent moon (a powerful symbol in pagan Britain), and also because it's made of that magical property, iron. There was even a mysterious Horseman's Society, complete with secret initiations. The members knew how to make a horse stop, rooted to the spot. This was called jading. On the other hand, they could also bring an unruly horse to them, called drawing.

Landowners and Labourers

The new machines meant poverty and starvation for them, and resulted in the Swing riots of 1830, when gangs of labourers broke the steam engines that were forcing them into the workhouse. In addition, many of the smaller farms were bought up by larger landowners. This was called enclosing and the enclosures created vast tracts of land for the wealthy, while doing away with the 20–30 acre subsistence smallholdings that originally dotted the landscape. A number of factors – low prices for farm goods, competition from overseas, an uncaring attitude from the gentry – resulted in the labourers having a harder life than ever. Typical meals consisted of bread and beer for breakfast and supper, with potatoes and greens for dinner, along with bacon perhaps twice a week. As one member of the gentry stated at the time, eight shillings was enough to keep a family in barley-bread and water for a week, and that was good enough for them!

Wealthy landowners, many of whom earned their money from the government, shipping or overseas investments, led a luxurious life, competing with each other to build the grandest mansions with lush, landscaped gardens. This was also a period of romantic interest in the classical world, as well as Britain's own history. The gentry loved to create follies, Doric temples and ready-built

Right:

Wealthy landowners had the time and money to create most of the white horses we see today. However, the advent of mechanisation meant an even harder life for the already down-trodden farm labourers. This painting depicts the Battle of Pyt House, between the Wiltshire Yeomanry and 400 farm workers during the Swing Riots of 1830.

# of this form of art

UFFINGTON • ALTON BARNES • HACKPEN HILL

The Alton Barnes Horse is best viewed from the Kennett and Avon Canal or from the road between Alton Barnes and Stanton St. Bernard. Situated above the village on the south slope of Pewsey Downs. The figure lies at the junction of a number of ancient trackways, including the Wansdyke, the Ridgeway and Tan Hill Way. It was carved in 1812 under the direction of Robert Pile, a local farmer. He paid a contractor £20 to do the work. The man made a sketch of what the final horse would look like, but vanished with the money before starting the work. He was later caught and hanged. The figure, 180 feet high and 165 feet long, is reputed to be a copy of the Cherhill Horse.

Above:

Hackpen Hill
White Horse, carved to
commemorate the
coronation of
Queen Victoria.

The Hackpen Hill Horse is best viewed by taking the minor road to Fiddler's Hill, opposite the turning for Broad Hinton on the A361 Avebury to Swindon road. It lies just beside the Broad Hinton to Marlborough road, and was carved by the parish clerk of Broad Hinton in 1838 to commemorate the coronation of Queen Victoria. By hill figure standards it is small at 90 feet long and 90 feet high.

The earliest horse figures are in harmony with the landscape, following the hills' soft rising and falling. A perfect example is the Uffington White Horse, although most agree now that it isn't a horse at all, it's more likely to represent a dragon, or even a cat, probably because of the two teeth-like projections at the bottom of its head. Later horses, all created or recreated in the 18th and 19th centuries, were less abstract.

During the latter half of the 18th century and the early 19th century, a new class of wealthy landowners emerged, due in part to the rise in the use of mechanisation on the farms, making them more profitable. Of course, this industrialisation had the opposite effect on the poor men who worked on the farms as labourers.

'ancient' castles to impress their friends. It is easy to imagine a local squire riding out in his carriage, passing the many farmhands along the way. He would bring with him an architect, and both, while sipping claret in their fine clothes and perfumed hair, would search the hills for one with the most pleasing prospect, and there lay out plans for another ancient monument.

The later horses were perhaps inspired by the paintings of George Stubbs (1724–1806). However the designers weren't impressed with the talents of Celtic horse carvers, and on at least two occasions had them recut to 'modern' standards, obliterating the ancient figures. Also, many of the horses changed shape because of the 'improvements' made during numerous scourings over the years.

Fortunately for the traveller, all of the hill figures in Wessex can be seen within a day or two, and the white horses in Wiltshire can be viewed in a day. It is interesting to find that every town near a white horse feels a close relationship with it, as though it were a tribal totem for that area, even if the figure is relatively new. As you view these hill figures, think back to a less hurried time, when the only noise on the roads was the creak of waggon wheels and the clatter of hoofs from that wondrous animal, the horse.

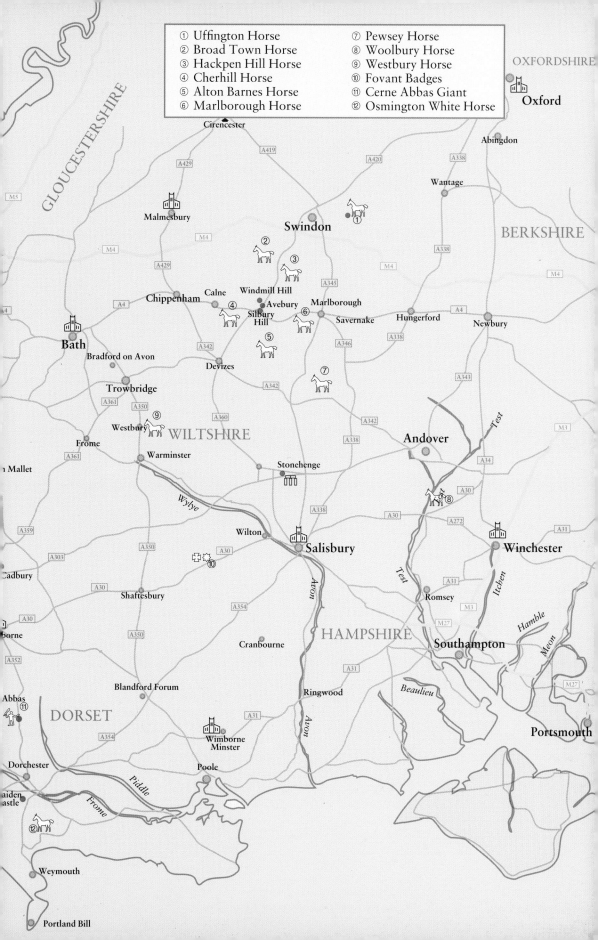

① Uffington Horse
② Broad Town Horse
③ Hackpen Hill Horse
④ Cherhill Horse
⑤ Alton Barnes Horse
⑥ Marlborough Horse
⑦ Pewsey Horse
⑧ Woolbury Horse
⑨ Westbury Horse
⑩ Fovant Badges
⑪ Cerne Abbas Giant
⑫ Osmington White Horse

OXFORDSHIRE

Oxford

Cirencester

GLOUCESTERSHIRE

Malmesbury

Abingdon

Wantage

Swindon

BERKSHIRE

Chippenham

Calne

Windmill Hill

Avebury

Silbury Hill

Marlborough

Savernake

Hungerford

Newbury

Bath

Bradford on Avon

Devizes

WILTSHIRE

Trowbridge

Westbury

Frome

Warminster

Stonehenge

Andover

n Mallet

Wilton

Salisbury

Winchester

Shaftesbury

Wylye

Test

Itchen

Hamble

Meon

Cadbury

Romsey

HAMPSHIRE

Southampton

Beaulieu

orne

Cranbourne

Portsmouth

DORSET

Blandford Forum

Ringwood

Abbas ⑪

Wimborne Minster

Avon

Dorchester

Poole

aiden astle

Piddle

Frome

⑫

Weymouth

Portland Bill

Great fairs, with as many as 30,000 people attending, were held on top of Uffington hill during the Middle Ages every 7 years up until 1857. It was one of the conditions for the Lord of the Manor, that he had to uphold the tradition of the scouring every seven years, and pay for the entertainment of the diggers. All of the local towns would join in to help. The Pastime, as it was called, was a great occasion, with booths and side-shows, pickpockets, pedlars and showmen. In 1843 Wombwell's circus was there, and had great difficulty getting the elephant van up the hill. Prizes were given for races and cheeses were rolled down the hill. There were all manner of contests, including grinning through a horse collar and even a smoke-a-thon, to see which woman could smoke the most tobacco in an hour.

There were double rows of stalls, each with musicians playing their loudest, on pipes and drums or whatever else they could get their hands on, to attract attention. Competing for eyes and ears were tightrope walkers, trapeze artists, circus and carnival performers of all types. There were also many different kinds of booth, including pubs, decked out in flower ribbons, complete with skittles at the back. In the middle of all this commotion was a

'WHITE HORSE HILL,
'BERKS, 1776.

'The scowering and cleansing of the White Horse is fixed for Monday the "27th day of May; on which day a Silver Cup will be run for near White Horse Hill, by any horse, &c. that never run for anything, carrying 11 stone,
the best of 3 two-mile heats, to start at ten o'clock.
'Between the heats will be run for by Poneys, a Saddle, Bridle and Whip; the best of '3 two-mile heats, the winner of 2 heats will be entitled to the Saddle, the second best the Bridle, and the third the Whip.
'The same time a Thill harness will be run for by Cart-horses, &c. in their harness and bells, the carters to ride in smock frocks without saddles, crossing and jostling, but no whipping allowed.
'A flitch of Bacon to be run for by asses.
'A good Hat to be run for by men in sacks, every man to bring his own sack.
'A Waistcoat, 10s. 6d. value, to be given to the person who shall take a bullet out of a tub of flour with his mouth in the shortest time.
'A Cheese to be run for down the White Horse Manger.
'Smocks to be run for by ladies, the second best of each prize to be entitled to a Silk Hat.
'Cudgel-playing for a gold-laced Hat and a pair of buckskin breeches, and Wrestling for a pair of silver Buckles and a pair of pumps.
'The horses to be on the White Horse Hill by nine o'clock.
'No less than four horses, &c. or asses to start for any of the above prizes.

The scouring of the Uffington Horse, from Hughes' Scouring of the White Horse *(1858).*

The Uffington Horse was regularly scoured despite the onslaughts of the Romans, Saxons, Danes and early Christian missionaries - so how marked were the differences between these peoples? Although wave after wave of migrations are conceded to have taken place, with warring tribes dispossessing each other's property and lands, miraculously the Uffington Horse was regularly dug out and filled with gleaming hunks of chalk. As with the Cerne Giant, its survival depended upon strenuous adherence to an unwavering custom. Although successive waves of invaders and settlers may have fought one another and differed in numerous ways, it seems that their common Indo-European ancestry acknowledged the primacy of the horse as a religious object.

large tent with the crude stage, next to the lord's tent. Everyone from fine ladies and gentlemen to gypsies were there. It is hard to believe that any actual work took place, but apparently it did.

When the scouring was under way, this song was sung:

> The owl White Horse want zetting to rights
> And the Squire hev promised good cheer
> Zo we'll gee un a scrape to kip un in shape
> And a'll last for many a year.

A fair sized horse near Marlborough only saw the light of day for a brief period in the summer of 1948. A ploughman, turning sods, accidentally uncovered the Rockley Down horse. There had been no mention of the animal before, and none of the locals had ever heard of it, either, even though it must have been hard to miss, at 120 feet long. Through neglect or on purpose, it soon reverted to grass.

Above:

The scouring of the hill figures was always a great occasion, since, by tradition, the Lord of the Manor had to pay for the entertainment of the diggers. With all the beer, spectacle and merry making, it's a wonder any work was ever finished!

There is no good view of the Marlborough Horse, although a fleeting glimpse can be seen on the A-4, next to Marlborough College Memorial Hall. Situated on a hill above the Kennett on the footpath to Preshute, it is rather small (62 feet long) and skinny, not the best artwork. There was no apparent motive for creating the figure, cut in 1804 by the boys of Mr Greasley's School. The horse is mentioned in the school song:

Ah, then we'll cry, thank God, my lads,
The Kennett's running still,
And see, the old White Horse still pads
Up there on Granham Hill.

The Pewsey Horse is best viewed from the drove road outside Pewsey where the Pewsey–Amesbury A345 turns off. There had been a horse on this spot for many years. The original was carved in 1785 under the direction of Robert Pile, who also designed the one at Alton Barnes. This first horse was reputed to have featured a rider. The horse that can now be seen is the second one on the spot, and is also the newest hill figure in Wessex. It is 66 feet long and 45 feet high, and was carved by the local fire brigade under

Top:

The new Pewsey White Horse. The original was reputed to have carried a rider on its back.

Right:

The Broad Town horse, although cut in 1867, had been lost until this decade.

Mr George Marples' direction in 1937, to commemorate the coronation of George VI. Since Marples had studied other horse hill figures, and realised how hard it was to date them, he even incorporated the year of the carving into the design.

The Broad Town Horse is on the road from Marlborough to Wootton Bassett, was cut in 1863, and best viewed from the Swindon–Bristol railway line. Claimed to have been created by William Simmonds in 1863, an old man at that time said it had been around for at least 50 years. It is 86 feet long by 61 feet high.

Below:
The Marlborough White Horse is one of the hardest to view, protected by a bank of trees, although a fleeting glimpse can be gained in the winter.

The Osmington Horse is best viewed from Weymouth Bay, or from the A353 between Preston and Osmington. At 323 feet high by 280 long, it's the largest of all the white horses, and the only one obviously meant to be seen from the sea. It was originally cut to be viewed by all the ships coming into the harbour of Weymouth Bay in Dorset. It indicated that the town was under royal patronage. There are three different theories as to how it came to be created. The first is that it was carved by a soldier to commemorate the visits made to Weymouth by George III and his brother the Duke of Gloucester. That seems like a lot of work for one person! The second is that it was made by engineers stationed in the area expecting a Napoleonic invasion. They must have had a lot of time on their hands since the invasion never occurred. The third is that it was carved by navvies celebrating the victory at Trafalgar (this theory is mentioned by Thomas Hardy). It is generally accepted that it is a depiction of King George III carved around 1815, although apparently there already was a horse on the hill in 1807, and only the king was added. Certainly the town was conscious of the effect of his visits, and went to great pains to capitalise on it but to little avail.

The Fovant Badges

The Fovant Regimental Badges are best viewed on the A30, about seven miles from Wilton. The badges are the only thing left to remind us of what was once an important military camp to which soldiers from all parts of the country came to train for active service in WWI. The area would have been a hive of activity, with men and military vehicles, a railroad, offices, hospital and even a cinema showing Buster Keaton and Charlie Chaplin films twice a night. British, American and Australians troops all inter-mingled and provided for plenty of excitement. Towards the end of the war, some of the Australians actually mutinied and became native, living in the hills and wood around the site. It also served towards the end of the war as a concentration camp for German POWs. At the end of the war it was one of the largest demobilisation camps in the country.

They were cut to be seen on the Shaftesbury to Salisbury road, the military badges were made around 1916 by men stationed at the huge training and mobility camps in the area before setting off for the Western Front. The first one was excavated by members of the London Rifle Brigade, who had just returned, wounded, from France. The practice caught on, and soon nearly all of the regiments were trying to out-do each other.

Below:

The Fovant Badges Society maintain twelve of the badges cut in the hillside near Fovant.

The chronology of the hill figures of Wessex

Uffington White Horse. First century AD? Berkshire.
Cerne Abbas Giant. Late second century AD? Dorset.
Gog and Magog. 1300 or before. Devon. Vanished.
Bratton White Horse. 1778. Wiltshire.
Cherhill White Horse. 1780. Wiltshire.
Marlborough White Horse. 1804. Wiltshire.
Alton Barnes White Horse. 1812. Wiltshire.
Osmington White Horse. 1815. Dorset.
Roundway Hill White Horse. 1845. Wiltshire. Vanished.
Hackpen Hill White Horse. 1848. Wiltshire.
Woolbury Horse. 1859. Wiltshire.
Broad Town White Horse. 1863. Wiltshire.
Inkpen Hill White Horse. 1868. Wiltshire. Vanished.
Fovant Military Badges. 1916–1919. Wiltshire.
Bulford Kiwi. 1918. Wiltshire.
Pewsey White Horse. 1937 (first cut 1785). Wiltshire.
Laverstock Panda. 1969. Wiltshire. Vanished.

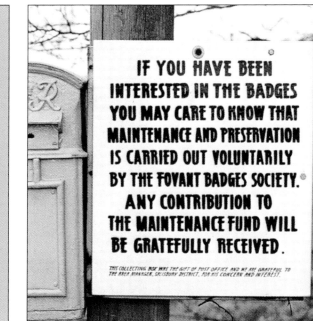

IF YOU HAVE BEEN INTERESTED IN THE BADGES YOU MAY CARE TO KNOW THAT MAINTENANCE AND PRESERVATION IS CARRIED OUT VOLUNTARILY BY THE FOVANT BADGES SOCIETY. ANY CONTRIBUTION TO THE MAINTENANCE FUND WILL BE GRATEFULLY RECEIVED.

THIS COLLECTING BOX WAS THE GIFT OF POST OFFICE AND WE ARE GRATEFUL TO THE AREA MANAGER, SALISBURY DISTRICT, FOR HIS CONCERN AND INTEREST.

We Shall Remember Them

This page:

Not all chalk figures are representations of horses or giants. These military badges cut in the hill below Chiselbury Camp on Salisbury Plain, are some of the newest hill figures of Wessex.

The badges, which took several months to make, were created by either digging a deep trench around the outline and filling it with chalk, or putting fresh chalk and other materials on top of the ground. They had to be worked on before dawn, because after that the hills were in constant use for rifle practice. After the morning's work, the men would toboggan down the hills on their shovels. By 1919 there were 20 badges, although not all survived.

They were allowed to become overgrown during WWII so that their shapes couldn't be used as markers to guide enemy planes. Some were restored in 1949 by the Fovant Home Guard Old Comrades, so that now there are twelve left that can still be seen. A Drumhead Service is still held on the first Sunday in July.

When viewed from east to west the Badges are:

Map of Australia;

The Royal Wiltshire Yeomanry, formed in 1794 when Mr Pitt, at the Bear Inn in Devizes, decided that the country needed a force to strengthen the internal defences of the country. First foreign action was in the Boer War. Also saw action in WWI in the Battle of the Somme, in WWII at Tobruk and the Battle of El Alamein;

YMCA;

6th City of London Regiment, formed in 1859 at a time of French aggression. It was volunteer, and so had no money for training, pay or uniforms. The men had to pay for the privilege of serving Queen Victoria. When WWII broke out, 90% of the members immediately volunteered for service. Action at Somme, Messines, Ypres, Pursuit to Mons, Ameins, Hindenberg Line. Also known as the Cast Iron Sixth;

Australian Commonwealth Military Forces. Prior to the outbreak of WWI, Australia said it would provide troops for whatever cause the British thought best. They served in France, Egypt, Suez Canal, Palestine, Italy and the Pacific. They sustained a large number of

Top row – left to right:
*7th City of London
Battalion;
Map of Australia;
The Bulford Kiwi;
Y.M.C.A.;
Royal Corps of Signals*

Middle row – left to right:
*6th Battalion London
Regiment;
Australian Imperial Force;
Royal Warwickshire
Regiment;
Wiltshire Regiment*

Bottom row – left to right:
Post Office Rifles;
Royal Wiltshire Yeomanry;
Devonshire Regiment;
London Rifle Brigade

casualties. Large numbers of them were in south Wiltshire for training or rehabilitation. In WWII they fought mainly in the Middle East and South Pacific, and also defended their home;

Royal Signal Corps;

Wiltshire Regiment, composed of two battalions, the 1st and 2nd. The 1st was formed in 1756 and served in the American War of Independence, the Sikh and Crimean wars, and in India and Burma during WWI. The 2nd was formed in 1824, took part in the British Expedition to China, served in most of the great battles in France in WWI. Served at Dunkirk in WWII and also in Palestine, Syria, Sicily and Italy. Nicknamed The Moonrakers, after the old Wiltshire tale;

London Rifle Brigade, formed as volunteers in 1859, served on the Western Front in WWI. Also served in North Africa and Italy in WWII;

Post Office Rifles, first formed in 1868, with recruitments coming originally from the London Post Office. Served in France in WWI with heavy losses, many Canadians among them;

Devonshire Regiment, raised in 1685 by the Duke of Beaufort. Fought in Canada, Scotland and Ireland in the 16th century. Also served in the Napoleonic Wars and in all major campaigns in both World Wars;

7th City of London Regiment, descended from the Trained Bands

of early Elizabethan times, served in South Africa in 1900s and Flanders during WWI, in WWII became the first S/L unit to bring down an enemy plane on British soil;

Royal Warwickshire Regiment, founded in 1674. Have seen action in a number of places throughout its history, including France in WWI and India, Burma and Normandy in WWII.

The Bulford Kiwi is best viewed from Bulford Barracks. Cut on Beacon Hill, north-east of Bulford and on the firing range, in 1918. It was made during the vogue of cutting badges by various regiments staying in the area during WWI and commemorates the occupation of Sling Camp by troops from New Zealand. Designed by Capt HM Clark, it's 420 feet long, with 'NZ' 65 feet high below the beak.

The Codford Rising Sun is part of the Fovant Regimental Badges. The rising sun badge was used by Anzac troops and was cut by the Australian Commonwealth Military Forces stationed around Fovant in 1916.

Australia, at Compton Chamberlayne, is also part of the Fovant group. This huge map of Australia and Tasmania was made in 1916 and restored in 1950.

The Laverstock Panda is best viewed (when scoured) about one mile north of Salisbury on the A30 Exeter road. Chalk graffiti that appeared overnight 24 January 1969, the 55 foot head of the panda is now barely discernible. UCNW is carved below it, most likely to mean University College of North Wales, whose mascot is the panda.

Top left:
Devonshire Regiment

Top right:
Royal Corps of Signals;
Wiltshire Regiment

Bottom (left to right):
Royal Wiltshire
Yeomanry;
Y.M.C.A.;
6th City of London
Regiment

Conclusion

Below:

Many of the hill figures of Wessex were cut in the 18th century, long before the advent of motor cars, radios and television. Instead, the tranquil sounds of horses, an indispensible part of life, were everywhere.

In all of human history, there has been the urge to alter our natural surroundings. Part of the reason for this has been to identify territory, so the earliest British farmers built burial mounds, the Celts following the tradition later by creating the Uffington White Horse.

Although most of the other hill figures weren't carved until the 18th and 19th centuries, the tradition of proudly proclaiming a territory (and the fact that they had the time and money to undertake such a project) was still carried on by wealthy landowners.

Even now, as we gaze upon these gleaming white monuments, we can almost imagine ourselves transplanted back to the time when they were first created. The harsh sound of the automobile engine is still a long way off; replaced by the steady clip-clop of hooves, the creaking of cart wheels and the friendly banter heard along the muddy roads. The air is filled with the smells of new-mown hay, hearth fires burning, the perfume of cattle and horses, fresh bread, ale and cheese.

There, high up on the crest of the hill, workers are stripping away the turf to reveal the white chalk underneath. The slowly forming figure will be enormous, visible for as far as the eye can see. What a grand sight the new white horse will make! It may be on the Lord of the Manor's land, and he may be paying for it.